D1518494

Abraham Lincoln

by Grace Hansen

ABDO
UNITED STATES
PRESIDENT BIOGRAPHIES
Kids

www.abdopublishing.com

Published by Abdo Kids, a division of ABDO, PO Box 398166, Minneapolis, Minnesota 55439.

Copyright © 2015 by Abdo Consulting Group, Inc. International copyrights reserved in all countries. No part of this book may be reproduced in any form without written permission from the publisher.

Printed in the United States of America, North Mankato, Minnesota.

052014

092014

Photo Credits: Corbis, Shutterstock, Thinkstock, © Daniel Schwen / CC-BY-SA-3.0 p.5, © User:Wknight94 / CC-BY-SA-3.0 p.21

Production Contributors: Teddy Borth, Jennie Forsberg, Grace Hansen

Design Contributors: Candice Keimig, Laura Rask, Dorothy Toth

Library of Congress Control Number: 2013953023

Cataloging-in-Publication Data

Hansen, Grace.

 Abraham Lincoln / Grace Hansen.

   p. cm. -- (United States president biographies)

ISBN 978-1-62970-085-4 (lib. bdg.)

Includes bibliographical references and index.

1. Lincoln, Abraham, 1809-1865--Juvenile literature. 2. Presidents--United States--Biography--Juvenile literature.   I. Title.

973.7092--dc23

[B]   2013953023

Table of Contents

Early Life

Abraham Lincoln was born February 12, 1809. He was born in Hardin County, Kentucky.

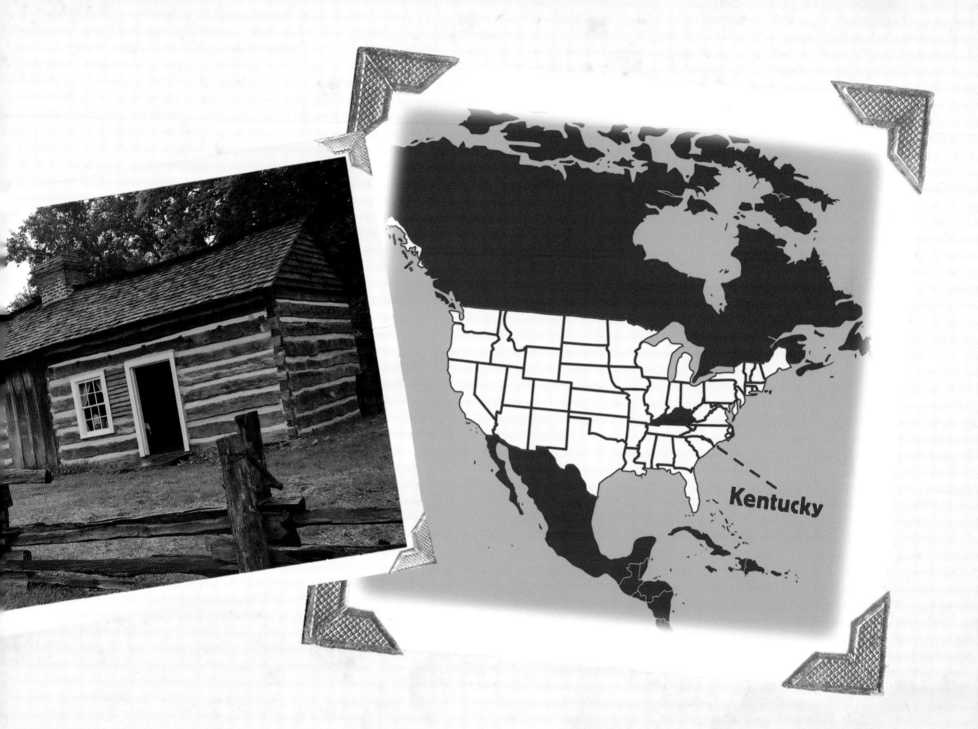

Kentucky

Lincoln had to work to support his family. He did not have much time for school.

Lincoln was smart. He

taught himself many things.

He worked in government.

He was also a lawyer.

9

Family

Lincoln married Mary Todd.

They had four boys.

Becoming President

Lincoln ran for Senate and lost. But his debates made him well known.

13

Presidency

In 1861, Lincoln became the 16th US president. Soon after, the **Civil War** began.

15

The war lasted for four years.

The North **defeated** the South.

17

In his second term, Lincoln planned to **reunite** the nation. But he would not be able to.

19

Death

On April 14, 1865 Lincoln went to Ford's Theatre. He was shot and killed while watching a play.